BRITAIN IN OLD P

AROUND
BAKEWELL

DAVID A. BARTON
& LAURENCE KNIGHTON

SUTTON PUBLISHING LIMITED

Sutton Publishing Limited
Phoenix Mill · Thrupp · Stroud
Gloucestershire · GL5 2BU

First published 1997

British Library Cataloguing in Publication Data
A catalogue record for this book is available from the
British Library.

ISBN 0-7509-1432-7

Typeset in 10/12 Perpetua.
Typesetting and origination by
Sutton Publishing Limited.
Printed in Great Britain by
Ebenezer Baylis, Worcester.

CONTENTS

The view from Barrett's Yard, Bakewell towards the tree-lined churchyard, *c.* 1915. The houses behind the North Church Street frontage have since been demolished. The women at the door are probably Mrs Hamilton and her daughter Phyllis with a friend.

INTRODUCTION

Derbyshire is a county of contrasts – from the pastoral lands of the south to the ruggedness of the Peaks, with the resultant feeling of the Midlands to the south and that of the North Country in the more Pennine areas. The eastern border with Nottinghamshire consists of coal measures beneath rich farmland. As a result of the Industrial Revolution, towns developed from small villages, although these now have an appearance of weariness. Sheffield and South Yorkshire now seem very close, owing to the all-prevailing motor car which has shifted the traditional focus from the old County Borough of Derby, now elevated to city status, once the administrative headquarters of the county.

Bakewell, nestling as it does around the parish church of All Saints, was quaintly described as 'the metropolis of the peak' in Pigot's guide of 1847. It is a town of the north when compared with the politeness of Ashbourne and is situated on an important historic crossroads. It is interesting to reflect that the through route via Ashford and Buxton did not develop until after the Ashford Buxton Turnpike Act of 1810: before that the main road passed through Tideswell. Now the north–south road is the A6 trunk road, which attracts too much traffic through the town to the detriment of the buildings and the well-being of the inhabitants.

In past times Bakewell presented a very different appearance from today, with even narrower streets and timber-framed buildings. Thatched roofs were not uncommon – a rating survey of 1847 shows sixty thatched dwellings; stables and other buildings were also thatched. Timber-framed buildings that survived were encased in stone. The opening of the railway in 1862 brought slates cheaply and quickly to the town and the surrounding area, but the last thatched cottages had their roofs replaced with tiles only after the Second World War. The old streets and lanes converged upon the area below the Old Town Hall in the present King Street, while a row of houses continued from the precursor of the post office into the present Rutland Square. This meant that the streets were rather narrow – a local myth asserted that when riding through town it was possible to touch the buildings on both sides of the road.

The modern layout of the town came early in the nineteenth century when the White Horse Inn was rebuilt as the Rutland Arms in about 1805 and Rutland Square was created. Plain but substantial buildings of distinction date from this period. In the mid-nineteenth century the local quarry, which produced lovely golden sandstone, was closed and the most durable gritstone, a grey, much more drab material, from the surrounding area was used instead. Much rebuilding then took place, especially of public buildings, schools and certain shops; although this was in the age of pioneering photographers the predecessors of the new buildings do not seem to have been recorded by the camera. Perhaps this was because Bakewell was a quiet reserved town and relatively few commercial postcards depicting it were issued. Some areas of towns and villages were never photographed – perhaps the subject was too everyday or mundane, while unfashionable streets were ignored. Finally, in 1920 the Duke of Rutland sold the vast majority of his Bakewell properties, some 200 lots.

They included two country residences, two gentlemen's residences and six licensed hotels or inns. At this time, His Grace gave to the town the recreation ground and the woods.

Ashford was once noted for the lead mines in its vicinity and its marble mill, where various marbles of many tints were polished. It is a charming village on the east side of the River Wye and used to be part of the Chatsworth estate. There is Duke's Drive, a pre-war bypass on the A6, as well as a much newer bridge and road primarily for stone traffic from the Buxton area.

The ancient upland village of Youlgrave (or Pommie, as it is fondly known in recognition of the local band of years past) stands high above the valley in the midst of fine limestone scenery on the River Bradford, a tributary of the Wye. Of independent character, the greater part of the village straggles along the long main street, which is dominated by the parish church of All Saints. The rambling seventeenth-century Old Hall, together with the adjacent Old Hall Farm, are noteworthy buildings. Youlgrave once enjoyed the distinction of being the largest village in the county without a railway station. The neighbouring township of Alport is small and delightfully situated at the junction of the River Lathkill and the River Bradford. It has unusually rewarding houses of the seventeenth and eighteenth centuries.

Rowsley is in effect two villages. Within the National Park is Great Rowsley, part of the Duke of Rutland's Haddon estate, its most distinctive building being the Peacock Hotel which has mullioned and transomed windows and a two-storey porch. Nearby are other pleasing buildings of the seventeenth and eighteenth centuries. The name Church Lane dates from the building of St Catherine's Church in 1855; before the construction of the new road this older way was the principal route to Bakewell. Little Rowsley was really Railway Rowsley – the oldest railway buildings of around 1850 are pure Chatsworth Estate Paxton design, as the Duke of Devonshire had interests in this small railway. Later on, Rowsley became a major railway depot and some sixty rather utilitarian houses were built along Chatsworth Road. The station saw much activity, with royal and ducal noble visitors travelling to and from Chatsworth while at holiday times crowds would arrive to visit the area and be tempted by tea and refreshments provided by the villagers. To add to the element of confusion, Little Rowsley was actually in the parish of Darley and later became part of the Urban District of Matlock.

Could the founders of the National Park ever have envisaged 22 million visitors per year to the park, or that the Bakewell Visitors' Centre would be visited by 175,000 people in 1996? There is no doubt that the National Park and Access to the Countryside Act of 1949 which set up National Parks has been responsible for conserving and protecting both Bakewell itself and the surrounding countryside. The Peak District National Park Authority, under a different name, was the first to be set up in 1951.

Older photographs serve to illustrate the changes – some good, some not so good – that have occurred over the years. Events and people are caught and frozen in an image – the formality of the posed photograph, proud people and scenes at school, people at play and at work, memorable views of the Carnival or Show, which meant so much to so many, are all included here. The farming scenes, too, evoke an earlier age. Scenes that are tranquil and peaceful are often in complete contrast to the same location today. If life for many was harder in the past, was it also more rewarding?

Thanks must be given to the mostly anonymous cameramen of the past for recording the various scenes, either by accident or design, as their invaluable visual record aids the local history student to appreciate the past more fully.

Laurence Knighton
Bakewell 1997

BAKEWELL

The more affluent visitor to Bakewell or locals returning with luggage joined the station bus operated by the Rutland Arms, which also ran to outlying districts of the town – the last passenger enjoyed a scenic tour! The bus was horse drawn until about 1916 and was withdrawn in October 1946. Here the driver, John Gannon, stands proudly by his vehicle.

An aerial view of the town, *c.* 1922. Perhaps it was a Monday as washing lines are to be seen and the stall market is in evidence.

Coombs Road photographed from Station Road, *c.* 1900. On the left is Woodbine Cottage, occupied by Mr T. Allsop, building contractor, and on the right is part of the Bridge Allotment Gardens, which was sold as building land in 1920 and is now one of Bakewell's numerous car parks.

A wedding group outside Woodbine Cottage, 2 April 1900. Tissee (Elizabeth) Allsop was marrying Joe Wain. Back row, left to right: three ministers, Grannie Allsop, Tom Allsop, Mr C. Morris (?), George Allsop. Front row: Mrs F. Percy, Katherine Wain, Joe Wain, Tissee Wain, Mrs Alice Morris, Rebecca Heath.

Another view of the wedding, this time in the garden with the wooded hillside behind. Among those present in this group are Mr Heath, Mrs Allsop, Mr Allsop, Rebecca Heath, Lucy Wallis, Cathie Wain, Charlie, Alice and Billie Wain, George Allsop, Florrie Davies, Will Hudson, Charles Wallis, Eva Wallis, Mr Newsome and Grannie Wallis (wearing bonnet).

Bakewell Union Workhouse was completed in 1841, the Union of Parishes in the area having been formed in August 1838. The clock and belfry cost some £80; sadly post-war works resulted in the removal of the attractive belfry but the original clock face remains, now driven by electricity. The works were given to the local museum but the weights were dropped within the masonry. The workhouse's front gardens were, until recent years, a real credit to the gardeners and formed an attractive feature of the town. It is now the Newholme Community Hospital, its patients housed in modern accommodation with very high standards of care and attention.

After exchanging some land with the Duke of Devonshire, John Barker was able to build the imposing Burre House in Holme Lane in about 1820. This photograph was taken before the alterations approved by the UDC in August 1896 were carried out; these included new stables at the rear of the house.

Trees have been planted in Scot's Gardens by the river to celebrate various events over the years. Here Mr C.R. Allcock, a member of the Scouts since 1910 and former president, plants a tree as part of the National Tree Campaign of 1975, watched by Ian Bright, Eddie Welch (Mayor of Bakewell 1975–6) and George Fearn, and several Scouts.

This attractive Edwardian postcard view of Bridge Street was published by Crowther Cox of Rotherham. The Queen's Arms was formerly the Durham Ox, and its landlord was George Ollivant, who became licensee in 1901. The pub has seen changes – the shop window has been replaced by a conventional one and the door moved to the other side. The houses opposite became shops over the years, including one which had Howard's Smithy immediately behind it.

The splendid, then modern, shop front of Wallis ironmonger's in Bridge Street, with members of the family outside. One could purchase almost anything here from dolly tubs to fireworks. The building is now occupied by Bagshaw estate agents and it is the only old building remaining in this part of the street.

The new Town Hall on the left had been completed in 1890 and in this view further redevelopment is about to take place: Critchlow's shop is about to be demolished, one of the posters reading 'Premises Closing Down'. The original intention was to build a new post office in Bath Street but at a public meeting held in February 1893 it was decided to build the Grammar School in Bath Street and the post office as near the centre of town as possible, replacing premises then occupied by Critchlow, Wyatt & Mountney.

The Anchor Inn, Coronation Day, 26 June 1902. It was run by the Briddon family for many years and the area between the Town Hall and the function room of the enlarged Wheatsheaf is still known as Anchor Square. A standard double-handled gallon measure marked 'Bakewell. Com. Derb. 1678' was found in the cellar here over one hundred years ago and preserved.

The market hall is of seventeenth-century origin; two walls at least contained open arches but were probably filled in during extension work in the eighteenth century. The stylish chimney stacks were demolished in modern times. The hall is pictured here between the wars; the sign MOTOR PARK says it all.

The east end of the market hall. From 1827 it was called the town hall: the lower floor was used as a wash house while the upper floor, which was taken out in 1858, was used as the Court Room. The end elevation became unstable and unsafe and in 1896 plans were put forward to rebuild it; one scheme had very large arches but the alternative was adopted. If only it could be reconstructed and restored to its original appearance! In the distance can be seen the horse bus to the station.

Bakewell Band pictured near the Peacock Hotel before a concert in the market place, 1942. Back row, left to right: -?-, Leonard (Penny) Birds, Herbert McGregor, Charlie Roper, Ron Parker, Jack Jones, Laurie Barker, John (Chitty) Marsden, Frank (Lumpy) Lomas, Charlie McGregor, Alf James, Charlie Bramwell, Cecil Alcock, Norman Robinson, RASC soldier. Front row: Bill Dickinson, Sam McGregor, Arthur Willis, Ken Frost.

The famous Bakewell Pudding Shop, originally run by the Wilson family, c. 1960. A second shop window has recently replaced a Georgian sash window which was itself a renewal of an old mullioned window similar to those on the first floor. In the distance is the market hall with its rebuilt gable end.

Denman's House, built in the early eighteenth century, is shown here as it was depicted in the billhead of Kay's Boarding School for Young Gentlemen. For some years after 1862 Lady Manners' School became associated with this private grammar school. It was sold in 1888 to Isaac Ash of Buxton, and in 1893 consideration was given to its possible conversion into tenements and shops, which were to be brought forward as far as the railings. Lady Manners' School was the grammar school founded in 1636 by Grace, Lady Manners of Haddon Hall. Today it is a grant-maintained co-educational comprehensive boarding and day school.

MR. KAY'S BOARDING SCHOOL FOR YOUNG GENTLEMEN,
BRIDGE STREET, BAKEWELL,
DERBYSHIRE.

ESTABLISHED IN 1850.

MR. WILLIAM KAY,

Head Master of the Grammar School; Licentiate of the Royal College of Preceptors; formerly Second Master of the Grammar School, Chesterfield; previously Assistant Master in the Collegiate Institution, Liverpool, &c., &c.,

ASSISTED BY HIS SON, MR. W. W. KAY,

AND QUALIFIED RESIDENT ENGLISH AND FOREIGN MASTERS,
RECEIVES
YOUNG GENTLEMEN AS BOARDERS,
AT FIVE GUINEAS AND UPWARDS PER QUARTER.

MRS. KAY'S BOARDING SCHOOL
FOR YOUNG LADIES,
BANK HOUSE, BATH STREET,
BAKEWELL, DERBYSHIRE.

ESTABLISHED IN 1868.

MRS. KAY,

Assisted by Governesses of ability and Visiting Masters,
RECEIVES YOUNG LADIES,
At Five Guineas and upwards per Quarter.

BANK HOUSE is large, commodious, and well adapted for the purpose of a Ladies' School, having Pleasure Grounds, extensive Gardens, and a good Play-ground, quite retired, for the use of the young ladies.
THE SCHOOL ROOM is a large detached up-stairs room, lofty, well lighted, and ventilated.

REFERENCES: Extended particulars of Terms, and other Information respecting the Schools, may be had on application.
NEW SCHOLARS CHARGED FROM THE TIME OF ENTRANCE.
Three months' notice prior to the removal of a Pupil required.

Bakewell is situated midway between Buxton and Matlock Bath, on the Midland New Route between London, Derby, Manchester, and Liverpool. Bakewell is proverbial for the salubrity of its situation, for the beautiful scenery of its neighbourhood, and in close proximity to Haddon Hall, Chatsworth, &c., &c.

School prospectus for Mr and Mrs Kay's businesses, 1868. The establishment for young ladies was originally in Bath Street but later moved to Bridge Street.

Scouts on manoeuvres somewhere in the meadows. Malcolm Sellors and Bill Briddon are among the group.

The 1st Bakewell Scouts at Weston-super-Mare, 1936.

Although of poor quality, this picture is of great interest. It shows Rutland Square on Coronation Day, 26 June 1902. A large flag flies over the Rutland Arms with other decorations and the letters ER. There is an air of expectancy: perhaps they are waiting for the proclamation of King Edward VII, as indicated in the various programmes of events for the day.

The Rutland Arms before the ballroom was constructed, *c.* 1895. Note the plain lampstand.

The Jacobean house in Rutland Square, *c.* 1920. This building was associated with the prosperous Gramer or Grammer family in the seventeenth century. Until its tragic demolition, 1936–8, it was known as the Clothing Store, as it had long been a drapery and clothing business. A Crow & Co. (late John C. Stroyan) advertisement in 1897 tells shoppers that it is 'the oldest established Business in the County . . . established 150 years'.

Rutland Square, photographed from the Rutland Arms, *c.* 1890. In those days people were more important than the motor car. This was evidently a gathering of the friendly societies and clubs, and a band was playing. On the right is the Jacobean house.

A fine view of Rutland Square. Note the ornamental lampstand to which finger-posts for Buxton and Matlock were affixed in 1905. The lampstand was erected in 1897 on the vicar's suggestion to commemorate the Queen's Jubilee.

Bath Gardens, *c.* 1956. The elegant railings that once stood on the wall between Rutland Square and Bath Gardens were taken away and melted down for the war effort during the Second World War. In about 1950 the footpath area was extended and this new wall was constructed with flower beds on top; the Second World War memorial is in the gardens behind. The absence of vehicles is unusual – perhaps the photograph was taken during the 1956 fuel crisis.

Rutland Square between the wars. The First World War memorial has replaced the Jubilee lampstand. The Rutland Tap 'Blood Tub' had been rebuilt and modernized and is now painted white. Older residents recall that the so-called Blood Tub was a rough house where fights regularly broke out. It was always the practice of the hotel to advertise the show.

Another view of Rutland Square between the wars, well before any roundabout was built! On the right is a Henry Hulley & Sons bus. This firm provided regular and much appreciated local services. A feature of the town in the past was the profusion of trees.

Hunting is one of the traditional country pursuits and the Harriers were established in 1848. Here Mr Hillyard of St Anselm's School greets two of his young scholars.

The Hunt moving off from the Rutland Arms. Traffic conditions now mean that the Hunt meets outside the Peacock Hotel in the Market Place.

R. Orme & Co.'s shop in Water Street, 1890. Mr Stanley Orme poses for the camera with his staff – and bacon at 6*d* per lb!

Various old buildings, including the Clothing Hall, were demolished between 1936 and 1938 to make way for the new premises of Orme & Co.

Described in the 1946 house magazine of R. Orme & Co. as 'a triumph of modern architectural design', this was the first stage of a road-widening scheme. The Royal Oak can be seen in the distance and a new pedestrian crossing in the foreground.

A SMALL LEAF TEA

with a

BIG   REPUTATION

BLENDED TO SUIT

THE DERBYSHIRE

WATER.

" . . . While now the
    country folk
Can sit beneath the
    spreading leaves
Of a mighty forest oak."

PACKED

SOLELY

BY THE

" PEAK "

GROCERS

The 1936 *Town Guide* has a similar advertisement for 'High Peak Teas, the finest value on the market, price 2/- per lb'. Orme's delivered everywhere in Derbyshire.

Bakewell Cricket Club, *c.* 1905. Included are three proud batsmen and three bowlers. Whites do not appear to be mandatory, or was it a practice night when the camera man came from Sheffield? Back row, left to right: W. Broomhead, C. Wallis, W. Fogg, H. Clark. Front row: H.Clulow, T. Gould, J. Townsend, -?-. The youth in the foreground is unknown.

Bakewell Football Club, 1904, photographed at the Derbyshire Cup Tie: Bakewell v. Belper at Matlock. (Bakewell lost.) Back row, left to right: Geo. Allsop, ? Large, Tom Mellor, Dick Clulow, Charley Marsden, ? Broomhead, Paul ? (of Derby County), ? Fisher. Seated are Sam MacGregor and Jim Turner. The club was founded in 1878.

Bakewell Night School football team, early 1900s. Back row, left to right: ? Agutter, B. Broombead, B. Boulsover, O. Clulow, S. Allcock. Middle row: B. Allsop, ? Clark, ? Smith. Front row: ? Thompson, ? Derbyshire, ? Turner, ? Thompson, ? Freeman. The football ground was on Cemetery Road, in a field now covered by houses.

Members of Bakewell Golf Club, photographed on Cup Competition Day, 18 September 1926. One of the club's founders was V.R. Cockerton, who served as Hon. Secretary for many years.

A mailcoach in Bakewell, photographed by James Gratton in the summer of 1881. Though mailcoach traffic collapsed with the coming of the railway, stagecoaches were still used for the ever-growing tourist traffic for trips around Chatsworth Park or to Buxton. The Rutland Stables have not yet been altered.

Rutland Stables, c. 1912. Increasing road traffic meant that complaints about the Stables were a regular feature of Council meetings at the turn of the century, and in 1903 it was decided to set the corner back by some twelve feet at a cost of £232 3s 2d, the work being undertaken by Allsop & Sons. This view of the Stables, together with a garage, is taken from a card headed 'From Wood & Woodiwiss, Bakewell', who were the proprietors. Mr Ernest Wood also ran the Rutland Arms from 1911 to 1938.

The Pigmarket and the start of Rutland Street photographed from a window of the Rutland Arms in 1888, before the shops were built. Note the profusion of Virginia creeper and the magnificent tree in the corner of the market.

The Rutland Garage

(opposite Hotel)

Has covered accommodation for 20 Cars.

Petrol, Oil, Tyres and Accessories are Stocked.

Provision is made for dealing expeditiously with all minor Repairs and Adjustments to Customers Cars.

Saloon Cars

May be hired for Touring, at Reasonable Charges.

E. & P. WOOD,

Proprietors.

An advertisement from a Rutland Arms brochure of 1925. The covered accommodation mentioned was reached through an arch between the various buildings.

Young Malcolm Sellors in the uniform of the Leicestershire Regiment during the First World War, ready to take on the enemy. He was a noted craftsman, particularly with stone slates and roofing, and was known throughout the county. The firm of H. & W. Sellors was established in 1850, although church records indicate that various members of the family had worked on the roof and steeple from the seventeenth century.

Rutland Terrace, built in about 1830, covered with Virginia creeper. At the end of the terrace a beech tree was later cut down after complaints about leaves on the pavement. The butcher's boy has no fear of being knocked down by road traffic! Prominent in the distance is the Congregational Chapel (now the Roman Catholic church), which was partially obscured by the building of a shop in about 1910.

Marchant Brooks & Co.'s office in the old Pigmarket, adjacent to Rutland Square, pictured between the wars. The firm ran the District Information Bureau on behalf of the council. Mr John Marchant Brooks was one of the principal founders of the town's Old House Museum.

Carnival Day, with a contingent from I.J. Rodgers Progress Works, probably in the 1930s. Of interest is the property at the corner of Rutland Street and Bath Street: pulled down in 1939, it consisted of a house, adjoining workshop and yard, and stables with five stalls. This property had been withdrawn for £490 at the Duke of Rutland's sale in 1920.

In the Coronation festivities of June 1911 four prizes – £5, £3, £2, and £1 – were on offer for the best illuminated displays of residences or business premises. Broomhead Plumbing in Rutland Street certainly went to town! The workshop and stores were behind the house and the premises are now occupied by Smith & Roper, architects. This short street is sometimes called Buxton Road, which it is not; Buxton Road actually begins at the junction with Bath Street.

Mary Broomhead,
SANITARY PLUMBER,
Glazier. Gas and Water Fitter,
RUTLAND STREET, BAKEWELL.

ESTIMATES GIVEN
FOR ALL THE ABOVE BRANCHES.

Hot ❧ Water ❧ Apparatus, ❧ Baths,
Lavatories, ❧ Water ❧ Closets,
and ❧ Pumps,
Supplied and fixed on the most improved principles.

BRASS FITTINGS
Of every description for Gas and Water.

**Authorised Agent to the Incandescent Gas Light Company
Limited.**

Six valid reasons why every gas consumer should
adopt the above system :

1. It saves half your gas bill.
2. It gives you treble your present light.
3. It can be attached to existing fittings.
4. The light is clean, cool, steady, brilliant.
5. It does away with the impurities of gas.
6. It is pleasant, simple, and economical.

An advertisement for Broomheads, 1897. The redoubtable Mary Broomhead ran the firm after the death of her husband.

Not quite Fern Grove but actually New Street decorated for carnival day, *c.* 1935. Community spirit was strong, and this area usually produced the best street decoration of all. These houses had been demolished, rather than refurbished, by 1939. There are new plans for houses to be built on the west side of the street in the near future.

The first of three views of the Pack Horse Bridge, which dates from 1664, pictured in about 1905. To the left is a Georgian house and to the right the stables of Holme Hall. The trees in the centre and on the right have since been removed.

The Pack Horse Bridge or Holme Bridge is featured in a card by J.A. Carrington of Bakewell, *c.* 1890. The house beyond the bridge had been demolished by the turn of the century. The river was the boundary between Bakewell and Holme, a township in the parish of Great Longstone. Portions of Lumford and Holme nearer the town were transferred to Bakewell Urban District Council in 1894 and 1903.

This view of the bridge was taken by the official Midland Railway photographer in about 1900, before the first of the new houses was built. In both this photograph and the previous one, the sylvan nature of the area is evident.

The staff of the D.P. Battery Co. at Lumford, 1901. This firm eventually became the major employer of the town and was well known for the manufacture of submarine batteries. They are shown in front of the old mill waterwheels dating from 1827 and 1832.

A fine example of the decorative letter heading used by the D.P. Battery Co. in 1911 is shown below.

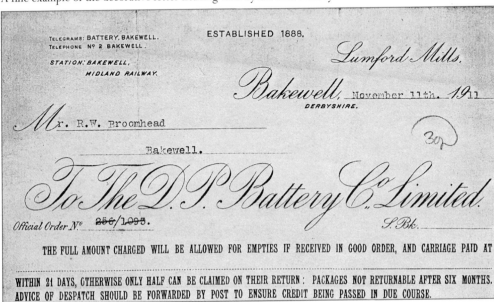

This aerial view shows the road to Ashford (the A6), *c.* 1925. Taken to show the D.P. Battery Co. and its surroundings, it is interesting today because there was then no Lakeside or building development along the A6, and the first batch of D.P. houses has yet to be built.

The weir and sluice between Ashford Lake and the mill pond for Lumford Mill *c.* 1935, which later became the works of the D.P. Battery Co.

The chemist's shop in King Street, *c.* 1910, when it was run by J.R. Thompson. It had been established in 1780 and is still remembered for its bottles and jars, lovely Georgian shop fittings and the mellowness of the gas lighting, which remained until the business ceased sometime after 1950.

JOHN R. THOMPSON, *(Late Coates)*

FAMILY AND DISPENSING CHEMIST,

Associate of the Pharmaceutical Society by Examination,

KING STREET, BAKEWELL.

Cod Liver Oil.   Tasteless Castor Oil.   Orange Quinine Wine.   Feeding Bottles.
Breast Pumps.   Invalid's Cups.   Trusses.   Hot Water Bags.   Nursing Aprons.
Hair Brushes.   Nail Brushes.   Tooth Brushes.   Dressing Combs.   Tooth Combs.
Toilet Soaps,   Medicinal Soaps.   Household Soaps.   Eau de Cologne.   Perfumes
(various).   Hair Restorers.   Pomades.   Hair Washes.   Tooth-ache Tincture.
Homœpathic Medicines.   Sponges (bath).   Sponges (toilet).   Sheep Dipping Compo
Extract Meat.   Essence Beef (tins).

CURTIS & HARVEY'S GUNPOWDERS.   EELEY BROS. SPORTING AMMUNITION SHOT, and every requisite for loading Cartridges.

PATENT MEDICINES: A variety of upwards of 500 always in stock.

Sole Agent for Celandine—the Cure for Corns.

This 1897 advertisement for Mr Thompson's establishment gives an idea of the multifarious goods on sale. How many chemists today would stock gunpowder?

The old Town Hall, *c.* 1948. Originally built in 1709, by this time it housed the fish and game shop of James Turner, while upstairs, reached by an outside staircase, was the Working Men's Club. In front was the Butter Market.

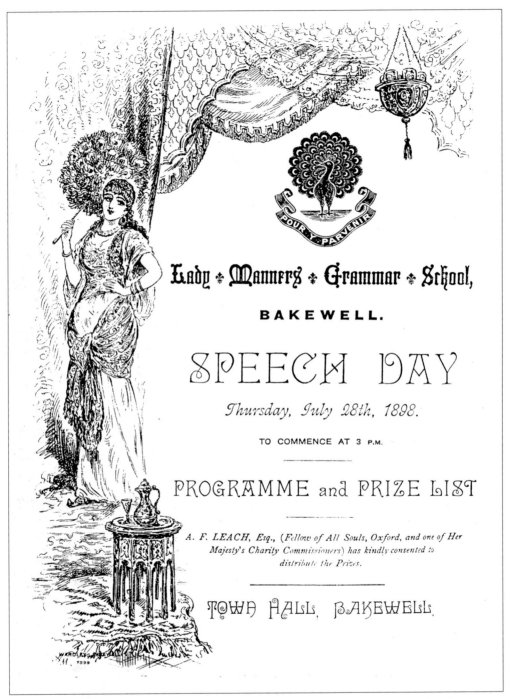

Lady ✦ Manners ✦ Grammar ✦ School,

BAKEWELL.

SPEECH DAY

Thursday, July 28th, 1898.

TO COMMENCE AT 3 P.M.

PROGRAMME and PRIZE LIST

A. F. LEACH, Esq., (*Fellow of All Souls, Oxford, and one of Her Majesty's Charity Commissioners*) *has kindly consented to distribute the Prizes.*

TOWN HALL, BAKEWELL.

A programme for the 1898 Speech Day at Lady Manners' Grammar School. At this time the school was in Bath Street.

The Almshouses (St John's Hospital) were founded in 1602 and these buildings date from 1709. This view was taken in 1948 before the old leaded window lights were replaced by modern reproductions. In the background can be seen the fire brigade bell tower on the old town hall; stone setts from Bath Street were used in its construction.

Interior of the Almshouses, c. 1900. This one was occupied by J. Waterfall, the 'Poet of the Peak', who sold sheets of poetry and church guides for a penny each. His curiosities are hung from the studding wall.

Barrett's Yard from North Church Street, *c*. 1915. In the distance is Tom Noton and his Midland Railway dray; his stables were adjacent. At the door are Mrs Bacon and her daughters, Alice and Flo. The properties on the right were regarded as substandard in 1936 and described as 'narrow houses, poor ventilation, no provision for washing clothes, pantry serves also for coals, uneven and poor floors, long detour to WC or pail closets as no back doors'. They were eventually demolished in about 1970.

North Church Street, *c*. 1915. Redevelopment of North Church Street and the area behind it took place after the enclosures when town land exchanges took place. In this century the properties in Sellor's Yard were considered substandard and were criticized by the Medical Officer of Health. Demolition was delayed by the Second World War and the subsequent housing shortage but it took place eventually in about 1958. Mrs Birley is at the door with her daughter Mable [*sic*] and two children.

The back of Sellor's Yard, *c*. 1915. Note the limited access to the garden and outside toilets.

The garden of Ivy House, South Church Street, looking across to the thatched cottages on the other side of the road, *c.* 1900.

A timeless photograph of the old thatched cottages in South Church Street, taken between the wars. These were the last properties in the town to have this style of roofing and it appears to be in good order. The demise of the top cottage was probably caused by the failure of the roof timbers rather than the thatch but it was reconstructed after 1960. Both cottages now have tiled roofs.

Revd Dr Edward Balston (1817–91). Formerly the headmaster of Eton, Balston was vicar of Bakewell from 1869 to 1891. He was also Rural Dean and Archdeacon from 1873. The new vicarage was built, to the design of Alfred Waterhouse, at Balston's own expense. He was also responsible for embellishing the chancel of Bakewell Church.

The parish church of All Saints from South Church Street; the trees, thatch and period windows have all since disappeared.

An ecumenical booklet, *Bakewell Churches* by W.G. Clarke, was published in 1928 by the Bakewell Press in King Street. At that time church and chapel schools were still quite separate, but all the clerics came together to be photographed for the book. Back row, left to right: Revd G.H. Wilson (Primitive Methodist), Revd F.T. Leaton (Congregationalist), Revd Mr Bansall (Church of England), Revd J.W. Vaughan (Wesleyan Reform), Father Firth (Roman Catholic). Front row: Mrs Brayshaw (Society of Friends), Revd E. Spink (Vicar of All Saints), Revd T.H. Sheriff (Wesleyan).

The chancel of the parish church of All Saints, as embellished by Archdeacon Balston, *c.* 1900. The designs on the walls have been subsequently painted over and the chancel redecorated.

All Saints' Church font, as depicted in a postcard by Geo. A. May of Bakewell, *c.* 1920. Old stalls can be seen on the left. The period woodwork has not survived well in the church.

A scene from the play *When We are Married* by J.B. Priestley, produced in 1973 by the Peacock Players, Bakewell's long-established amateur drama group. Left to right: Robin Gregory, Hilda Little, Margaret Blakeway, Leonard Twigg, Sue Stones and Allan Eaton.

Poet and Pheasant by Willis Hall and Lewis Jones was produced by the Peacock Players with the assistance of the Bakewell Silver Prize Band in March 1963. Left to right: Hazel Fletcher, Keith Mounsey, Cyril Mounsey (seated), Ian Caudewell, Margaret Blakeway, Olga Jones. Bandsmen: Wilf Hulley, Carl Tuck, George Fern, Len Birds, Billy Buer, Ken Frost.

The Conservative Club Presentation Night to award prizes to the winners of pre-Christmas 'Knockout' competitions, *c*. 1950. Left to right: Ben Kay, Martin Spencer, Cecil Maylin, George Hawley, Leslie Hodges, Richard Cockerton, Bill Hall (behind), Eric Robertson, the Duke of Devonshire, Joe Frost, Ernie Daniels, C. Hopkins, Len Mosley, Dick Mellor and Bill Flewitt.

Bakewell British Legion dinner, early 1950s. Left to right: Harold Mansfield, -?-, Charlie Mills, Dick Allcock, Wilf Quarnby, Ronald Knighton, -?-, -?-, Father Judd MC, Arthur Groom. Seated: Maurice Barker (?), -?-, T.A. Hughes, Arthur Smith.

The *Derbyshire Times* described the events of 1924 as 'A huge success. A really wonderful carnival with wonderful tableaux'. This was the first of Bakewell's larger carnivals and, then as now, it was very much a community occasion. This tradesmen's turnout by Thomas Smith & Sons of Holme Bank Mine won the third prize of 10*s*.

Another view of the 1924 carnival. 'Old Bill' received the third prize of 15*s* in the tableaux section.

Fancy dress entries at the 1934 carnival.

Another tableau from the 1930 carnival.

Described on this 1910 postcard produced in Scarborough as Bakewell – Old Bridge, this is the bridge over the mill stream adjacent to the Rutland Works timber yard. This was the ancient route towards Beeley but is now heavily used to reach the car parking areas and show ground.

Bakewell Show, 1930s. One of the highlights of Bakewell's year is the show, which takes place in August. Here Airedale terriers are being exhibited.

Bakewell Show was founded as long ago as 1819 and moved to this site in 1926. The house Brooklands is in the far background. This is another of the *Sheffield Telegraph* photographs taken before the war when hats were still almost mandatory.

In 1960 Bakewell Show was honoured by the presence of the then Prime Minister, Harold Macmillan, seen here with the Duchess of Rutland (left), the Duke of Rutland (centre), and the Duchess of Devonshire.

Winners in the goat class waiting to be presented with cups and prizes by the Duchess of Rutland.

Judging the dairy shorthorn in-calf class at Bakewell Show, 1955.

Comparing birds in the poultry section, Bakewell Show, 1950s. Left to right: -?-, Herbert Slack, -?-, Fred Sellars, Joe Mackfall, Trevor Slack.

Netball was introduced at Lady Manners' School in 1908, with the encouragement of the headmaster's wife, Mrs Jemmett. This picture was taken on 14 July 1909, the occasion when class Vb won 14 goals to 1 against the Junior Pupil Teachers.

Lady Manners' School netball team, *c*. 1968. Back row, left to right: Janice Crabb, Rachel Cluskey, Josephine Maltby. Front row: Fiona Duffield, Beverley Rookes, Jane Hudson, Deirdre Barton (now Coleman), Christine Andrew.

Lady Manners' School girls' cricket team, 1909.

Lady Manners' School boys' football team, *c.* 1909. They are pictured by the Tufa Grotto in Bath Gardens, which was removed after the First World War.

The formal opening of the War Memorial Library at Lady Manners' School, November 1938. Left to right: Mrs Mylechreest, Mr H.C. Brooke Taylor, Revd D.E. Gilmore (Chairman of the Governors), Mr F.W. Thompson, the Duke of Rutland, Mr A.E. Filsell (Headmaster), Mr A. Carrington, Mrs Coward, Mr A.R. Brand.

The headmaster and staff of Bakewell Church of England School, 1912. Back row, left to right: Mr R. Allcock, Miss Maddon, Mr George, Miss Radford, Mr Slater, Miss Mellor. Middle row: Miss Mellor, Miss Salt, Mr Sydney Allcock (headmaster), Miss Salt, Miss Rose. Front row: Miss Eyre, 'Pat', Miss ?. The young Dick Allcock (back row, left), later became the headmaster and a noted local historian.

Staff and clergy of Bakewell Methodist School, c. 1962. Left to right: Revd S.J. Slater (Methodist minister), Mrs Holland, Mr Mold, Miss Shannon, Mr Dunsford (headmaster), Mr Hawley, Miss Hallam, Revd P. Pilkington (curate).

An elementary cookery class at Bakewell Centre, July 1933. Mrs Marshall (née Alice Palfreyman) says, 'We made the pinafores and caps ourselves. They had a buttercup design.' Back row, left to right: E. Sheldon, E. Carroll, N. Swallow, J. Turner, M. Birley, F. Clark; ? Bennett. Middle row: B. Carter, A. Bond, E. Gratton, I. Noton, A. Palfreyman, H. Barnes. Front row: J. Smith, A. Hallows, B. Smithurst, A. Ashley, Mary Mellor.

Pupils from Bakewell Church of England School on a school trip to York enjoying a boat trip on the River Ouse to the Bishop's Palace, c. 1930. Included in the picture are Norman Rose, Joe Gregory, Billy Hamilton, Beattie Bradshaw, Joan Willis, Olive Clarke, Margaret Siddons, Hilda Robinson, Joan Turner, Rene Peters, Jean Watts, Margaret Birley and Rita Howard.

Passive resistance in Bakewell. Strong feelings were aroused by the Education Act of 1902, which required Nonconformists to contribute through local rates to the upkeep of Anglican schools. The more extreme opponents refused to pay the rates and this picture shows goods being taken in lieu of rates from a house in Mill Street (now Buxton Road). These would later be sold at auction to raise the money, but were often bought by friends and restored to their owners.

Before various preventative measures were taken, such as alterations to river banks and weirs, low-lying areas of the town used to flood during rainy periods or when heavy snow melted. This is Milford Bridge in February 1946 with Needham's Garage (built in 1910) in the background. If the photographer had stepped forward he would have fallen into the mill stream.

A charming Edwardian postcard depicting Milford Bridge leading to Castle Street, before the houses were built.

Milford, *c.* 1930. The houses are still not built.

Music classes at Bakewell Church of England School, *c.* 1939.

Pupils at Bakewell Church of England School, *c.* 1940.

Mr and Mrs W. Storrs Fox. Mr Storrs Fox (1860–1951) founded St Anselm's preparatory school at Bakewell in 1888 and was headmaster there until his retirement in 1921.

St Anselm's School in 1894.

One of the classrooms at St Anselm's before the First World War.

Boys from St Anselm's enjoying winter sports with a friend in Strange Road between the wars.

Interior of Bakewell station signal-box, April 1960. The signalman has 'pulled off' levers number 8, 9 and 10 to allow passage of an Up train. The levers painted with black and white chevrons are for detonator placers. The box opened in 1921 and was closed in July 1968.

View of the Down platform at Bakewell station, looking north, *c*. 1900. A goods train is shunting in the yard. The glass verandah and roofs were the idea of Sir Joseph Paxton.

Timber arrives at Bakewell station from Oxford on the GWR, *c*. 1906. The wood was unloaded on to timber drays for conveyance to Rutland Works, a large site on the east side of the river. The saw mill and stacking areas were run by Mr Robert Smith.

An Up express hauled by 4–4–0 Compound no. 1052 entering Bakewell station during the winter of 1947. Most of the glass has gone from the roof as a result of poor maintenance during the war and the difficult conditions afterwards. The bookstall of W.H. Smith still remains, although it is no longer used.

A proud moment at Bakewell station. This is the presentation of the Best Kept Station and Garden Award in 1960. Left to right: -?-, -?-, Noel Sims, G.A. Abbiss, David Winckle, W.P. Clarke, -?-, George Doxey, Arthur Mercer, Raymond Percival and John Hurst.

Murdock McKay of Bakewell operated bus services to Sheffield as well as locally to Ashford, Tideswell and Longstone, using charabanc-type vehicles. The Sheffield route was taken over by the Corporation in 1925. NU 2214 was a Crossley vehicle built in Stockport, which may have been ex-military, and R 8890 was a Fiat.

A Tilling Stevens TS 3 vehicle passing Whatstandwell Bridge on its way to Bakewell, c. 1920. Apparently this Trent service initially ran on Fridays and Saturdays only in the summer period.

A gymnastics display by boys of the athletic club run by Mr Malcolm Sellors, *c*. 1930. Like its counterpart the Boys' Brigade, the club was a useful initiative for keeping boys fit and out of trouble.

Crowds gather to watch the greasy pole contest over the river at the recreation ground at Carnival Time, *c*. 1948. Mr Sellors evidently triumphed.

This drawing by the late Dick Allcock shows the Primitive Methodist Chapel in Water Street, which was built in 1891 and represented the culmination of the efforts of Joshua Barrett and Charles Critchlow to establish Primitive Methodism in Bakewell. Membership lists show that a Primitive society existed in Bakewell in 1836 but it was not until 1870 that it became popular. The building was converted to a dairy in the 1960s and is now a newsagent's.

A stylized and rather elegant engraving of Bakewell Cemetery. Consecrated in 1858, it has two chapels, one for Anglicans and one for Nonconformists.

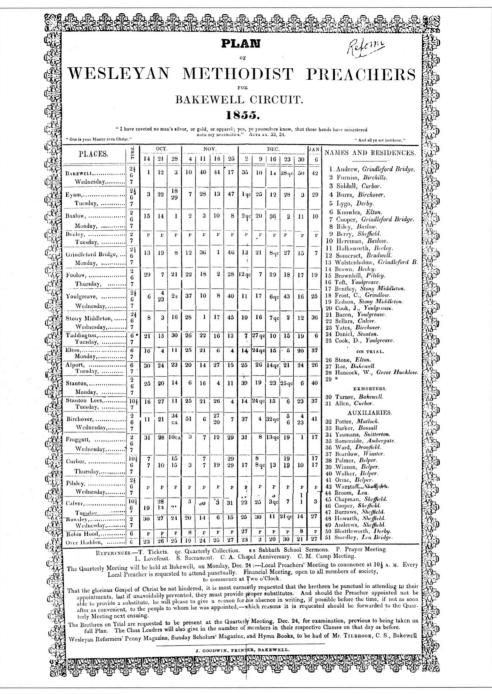

PLAN
OF
WESLEYAN METHODIST PREACHERS
FOR
BAKEWELL CIRCUIT.
1855.

"I have coveted no man's silver, or gold, or apparel; yea, ye yourselves know, that these hands have ministered unto my necessities." ACTS xx. 33, 34.

" One is your Master even Christ."   " And all ye are brethren."

PLACES.	TIME	OCT 14	OCT 21	OCT 28	NOV 4	NOV 11	NOV 18	NOV 25	DEC 2	DEC 9	DEC 16	DEC 23	DEC 30	JAN 6
BAKEWELL,	2¼/6	1	12	3	10	40	44	17	35	10	1s	38qc	50	42
Wednesday,	7													
Eyam,	2¼/6	3	22	18/29	7	28	13	47	1qc	25	12	28	3	29
Tuesday,	7													
Baslow,	2/6	15	14	1	2	3	10	8	2qc	20	36	9	11	10
Monday,	7													
Beeley,	2/7	r	r	r	r	r	r	r	r	r	r	r	r	r
Tuesday,	7													
Grindleford Bridge,	2¼/6	13	19	8	12	36	1	46	13	21	8qc	27	15	7
Monday,	7													
Foolow,	2/6	29	7	21	22	18	2	28	12qc	7	29	18	17	19
Thursday,	7													
Youlgreave,	2¼/6	6	4/23	2s	37	10	8	40	11	17	6qc	43	16	25
Wednesday,	7													
Stony Middleton,	2¼/6	8	3	16	28	1	17	45	10	16	7qc	2	12	36
Wednesday,	7													
Taddington,	6*	21	15	30	26	22	16	13	7	27qc	10	15	19	6
Tuesday,	7													
Elton,	6/7	16	4	11	25	21	6	4	14	24qc	15	5	20	37
Monday,	7													
Alport,	6/7	30	24	23	20	14	27	15	25	26	14qc	21	24	26
Tuesday,	7													
Stanton,	2/6	25	20	14	6	16	4	11	39	19	23	25qc	6	40
Monday,	7													
Stanton Lees,	10½/7	16	27	11	25	21	26	4	14	24qc	15	6	23	37
Tuesday,	7													
Birchover,	2/6/7	11	21	34/CA	51	6	27/20	7	37	4	32qc	5/6	4/23	41
Wednesday,	7													
Froggatt,	2/6	31	28	10cA	3	7	19	29	31	8	13qc	19	1	17
Wednesday,	7													
Curbor,	10½/6	7		15		7		29	8		19			17
Thursday,	7	7	10	15	3	7	19	29	17	8qc	13	12	10	17
Pilsley,	2¼/6	r	r	r	r	r	r	r	r	r	r	r	r	r
Wednesday,	7													
Calver,	10½/6	19	28/13	21	3	30	3	31	22	25	3qc	7	1	3
Tuesday,	7													
Rowsley,	2/7	30	27	24	20	14	6	15	25	30	11	21qc	14	27
Wednesday,	7													
Robin Hood,	6/7	r	r	r	8	r	r	8	r	r	r	8	r	
Over Haddon,	6	23	26	25	19	24	25	27	23	2	20	30	21	27

NAMES AND RESIDENCES.

1 Andrew, *Grindleford Bridge.*
2 Furniss, *Birchills.*
3 Siddall, *Curbor.*
4 Burrs, *Birchover.*
5 Lygo, *Derby.*
6 Knowles, *Elton.*
7 Cooper, *Grindleford Bridge.*
8 Riley, *Baslow.*
9 Berry, *Sheffield.*
10 Hereman, *Baslow.*
11 Halksworth, *Beeley.*
12 Somerset, *Bradwell.*
13 Wolstenholme, *Grindleford B.*
14 Brown, *Beeley.*
15 Brownhill, *Pilsley.*
16 Toft, *Youlgreave.*
17 Bentley, *Stony Middleton.*
18 Frost, C., *Grindlow.*
19 Eedson, *Stony Middleton.*
20 Cook, J., *Youlgreave.*
21 Bacon, *Youlgreave.*
22 Sellars, *Calver.*
23 Yates, *Birchover.*
24 Daniel, *Stanton.*
25 Cook, D., *Youlgreave.*

ON TRIAL..
26 Stone, *Elton.*
27 Roe, *Bakewell.*
28 Hancock, W., *Great Hucklow.*
29 *

EXHORTERS.
30 Turner, *Bakewell.*
31 Allen, *Curbor.*

AUXILIARIES.
32 Potter, *Matlock.*
33 Barker, *Bonsall*
34 Yeomans, *Snitterton.*
35 Somerside, *Ambergate.*
36 Ward, *Dronfield.*
37 Beardow, *Winster.*
38 Palmer, *Belper.*
39 Winson, *Belper.*
40 Walker, *Belper.*
41 Orme, *Belper.*
42 Wagstaff, *Shottle Urk.*
43 Broom, *Lea.*
44 Chapman, *Sheffield.*
45 Cooper, *Sheffield.*
46 Burrows, *Sheffield.*
47 Howarth, *Sheffield.*
48 Andrews, *Sheffield.*
49 Shuttleworth, *Derby.*
50 Smedley, *Lea Bridge.*

REFERENCES.—T. Tickets.   qc. Quarterly Collection.   s s Sabbath School Sermons.   P. Prayer Meeting.   L. Lovefeast.   S. Sacrament.   C. A. Chapel Anniversary.   C. M. Camp Meeting.

The Quarterly Meeting will be held at Bakewell, on Monday, Dec. 24:—Local Preachers' Meeting to commence at 10½ A. M. Every Local Preacher is requested to attend punctually. Financial Meeting, open to all members of society, to commence at Two o'Clock.

That the glorious Gospel of Christ be not hindered, it is most earnestly requested that the brethren be punctual in attending to their appointments, but if unavoidably prevented, they must provide proper substitutes. And should the Preacher appointed not be able to provide a substitute, he will please to give a reason for his absence in writing, if possible before the time, if not as soon after as convenient, to the people to whom he was appointed,—which reasons it is requested should be forwarded to the Quarterly Meeting next ensuing.

The Brethren on Trial are requested to be present at the Quarterly Meeting, Dec. 24, for examination, previous to being taken on full Plan. The Class Leaders will also give in the number of members in their respective Classes on that day as before.

Wesleyan Reformers' Penny Magazine, Sunday Scholars' Magazine, and Hymn Books, to be had of Mr. TILBROOK, C. S., Bakewell.

J. GOODWIN, PRINTER, BAKEWELL.

This is a preaching plan of the Bakewell Wesleyan Reformers. Widespread disaffection in the Wesleyan Church was brought to a head by the expulsion of three ministers in 1849. Many Wesleyans resigned in sympathy, and many more were expelled for expressing sympathy, both locally and nationally. They continued to call themselves Wesleyans, as they considered themselves to have been unjustly expelled. In 1859 the Wesleyan Reform Union was formed and the Wesleyan Reform Circuit survives to this day, although Bakewell Chapel has now been closed.

Members of the Wallis family pose for the photographer at Haddon Villa, The Avenue, *c.* 1910.

The question here should be, where is this? The almost Dutch-style dormer windows look very prominent but are rather hidden at the side of the Holme Hall, which was built by Bernard Wells in 1626.

A trade turn-out at Bakewell Show some time between 1920 and 1925, when it was still held on the Rutland recreation ground. This float could equally as well have taken part in the carnivals of the 1920s when horse power was still very much in evidence. *Kelly's Directory* of 1932 lists Joseph Mansfield as a hardware dealer in Church Alley.

The display stand of Mary Broomhead & Sons of Rutland Street at an exhibition in the Town Hall (*see* p. 33). This plumbing firm was established in 1785 and only ceased business after the Second World War. It would be interesting to know which other companies exhibited on this occasion.

Pupils of Boys' Secondary School, Bakewell, 1954. Back row, left to right: J. Banks, C. Turner, P. Wood, J. Simpson, E. Tindall, T. Cantrell, I. Cox, R. Fishwick, J. Holmes, P. Melland, H. Dearing, A. Wilton, -?-. Third row: J. Billinge, ? Gregory, S. Burer, H. Fletcher, K. Moore, D. Hascock, R. Carman, M. Nadin, F. Morton, R. Birdikin, L. Udall, ? Marsden, M. Hibbs. Second row: D. Sudbury, ? Hodgkinson, ? Gilbert, ? Betney, M. Robinson, S. Birds, W. Haslam, J. Wragg, C. Worsencroft, J. Ball. Front row: -?-, ? Morton, -?-, D. Wragg, P. Rogers, M. Taylor, A. Boam, I. Wright, B. Eades.

An idyllic summer's day by the river at Bakewell.

Jack and Jean Sellors pictured in 1934 at Milford before the houses were built.

Here 4–6–0 no. 45408 runs through Bakewell station, *c.* 1950, before the removal of the up side veranda roof. This picture was taken from the overbridge, a vantage point enjoyed by train enthusiasts of all ages over the years.

Visitors who arrived by train were greeted with this view of the town from Station Road. Again the profusion of trees is most noticeable, as are the dominating tower and spire of the parish church.

A mother and son negotiate the snowbound Hassop Road in 1947. The station is just visible in the distance. The boy, Laurence Knighton, is the co-author of this volume.

The Bakewell road to Ashford (the A6), photographed by the Midland Railway for display in carriage compartments, *c.* 1900. The road has since been widened.

ASHFORD & HASSOP

Ashford was the centre of the black marble industry, using locally quarried materials to produce finely inlaid ornamental work. This view, uncluttered by modern development, shows the medieval Church of Holy Trinity, which was almost completely rebuilt between 1868 and 1870 by J.M. and H. Taylor.

These two charming pictures show Ashford village in a period when life was more leisurely. The taller building in the centre of the lower picture is the Devonshire Arms, photographed at the turn of the century.

The Rookery, Ashford. Half hidden under its mantle of ivy, this elegant residence was occupied in 1895 by Mrs Agnes Sorby. The lawn runs down to the River Wye and behind the house is the old Buxton road, which has now been bypassed.

Known locally as the Bobbin Mill, this water mill in Ashford was built in 1878 and was closed in about 1931. It was reopened during the Second World War when it was used for the bailing of paper and tins.

The Bramwell family, complete with doll's perambulator, pictured at Ashford in about 1890.

Leonard and Elizabeth Bramwell, *c.* 1890. The pram seems more like a child's chariot than a baby's pram.

A procession headed by the local band has just passed the Top Pump, Ashford, the small building on the right. This was probably a church or school feast day.

A group of local worthies outside the Devonshire Arms, Ashford, *c.* 1903. This may be a friendly society gathering.

The north end of Duke's Drive in Ashford. The construction of this new road enabled the A6 to bypass the village of Ashford. The old road ran behind Marble Cottage, now much altered. Oh for those traffic-free days!

The official opening of the War Memorial Institute in 1932 by the Prince of Wales, accompanied by the Duke of York (later George VI) and the Duke of Devonshire. The Prince is shaking hands with Mr Herbert Wright, and waiting to be presented are Ernest Wright, Edgar Slaney and James Herbert Slaney. In the foreground (left) is County Councillor Arthur Marsden. Four miners from Youlgrave who were among the rescuers at the Mawston Mine disaster were also presented to the Prince.

Great Longstone station, looking south. This station always had prize-winning gardens. Originally called Longstone, its name was later changed to Great Longstone for Ashford.

The fernery at Thornbridge Hall, near Great Longstone. Thornbridge Hall was a Georgian house which was extensively altered in 1871 and in 1897 Charles Hadfield designed its spectacular neo-Tudor exterior. It was noted for its splendid gardens. After the Second World War it became a college of education.

An accident involving an empty wagon train at Rowland Road bridge near Longstone, *c.* 1900. The wagons were for locomotive coal and included an obsolete dumb-buffered vehicle, which crashed on to the highway.

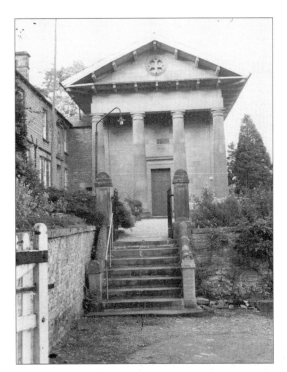

All Saints' Roman Catholic Church, Hassop. The small township of Hassop contains this rather elegant church. Built between 1816 and 1818, it was designed by Joseph Ireland for the Eyre family. The work was supervised by Ireland's pupil, J.J. Scoles, who later became one of the leading Catholic architects of the nineteenth century. Inside is an elaborate altar made of Sicilian marble.

This former farmhouse, now much restored, stands between Hassop station and Birchills. An almost hidden stone causeway runs from the house to Baslow Road across the fields. This photograph was taken in about 1940.

Troops of the Royal Army Medical Corps at Hassop station during the First World War. The Edensor Inn a few miles away was used as a convalescent hospital.

Staff at Hassop station, *c.* 1937–8. Eddie Mellor (left) later became a signalman at Haddon and Rowsley. Bob Thorpe, later signalman at Monsal Dale, also ran Cressbrook post office for many years, because of which he once attended a garden party at Buckingham Palace.

ALPORT

A small hamlet between Bakewell and Youlgrave, Alport was deprived of its only pub when the Boarding House Hotel became a private house in about 1928; it was demolished in 1937 for road widening.

Alport, before the road was widened.

Alport, 1930s.

The Boarding House Hotel, Alport.

Widening the bridge at Alport in 1937.

A postcard view of Alport from the 1930s.

Another view of Alport from the 1930s before the road was widened.

Haymaking at Haddon Fields Farm, Alport, 1916. Left to right: Marjorie Clarke, Polly Walker, Mrs Walker (from Nottingham), Charles Birds, Anthony Walker.

Workers at Haddon Fields Farm, *c.* 1956. Left to right: Willie Brassington, Robert Walken, Thomas Walker.

Scythemen at Haddon Fields Farm, *c*. 1920. Left to right: Anthony Walker, Noel Walker, Thomas Walker.

This seems to show a farm visit to Haddon Fields Farm, *c*. 1932. There are two hikers on the left while the cart is full of children and adults. The man leading the horse is Noel Walker.

Sheep dipping at Haddon Fields Farm, early
1930s. Left to right: Thomas Walker, Anthony
Walker, Albert Darby, Noel Walker.

Noel Walker and Thomas Walker preparing to shear the Suffolk sheep at Haddon Fields Farm, *c.* 1920.

Anthony Walker and Thomas Walker shearing the Suffolk sheep at Haddon Fields Farm, 1930s.

Thomas Walker inspecting the fleeces at Haddon Fields Farm, 1930s.

YOULGRAVE

Described by Bulmer's Directory in 1895 as the seat of a considerable mining population, Youlgrave lies some 3 miles south-west of Bakewell. The church of All Saints was described by Nikolaus Pevsner as one of the most impressive in Derbyshire. It was thoroughly restored by Norman Shaw between 1869 and 1870; the work included the installation of new pews, stalls, lectern, pulpit and reredos, with an important stained glass window by Edward Burne-Jones at the east end.

Bankside, Youlgrave, *c*. 1892.

The Fisherman's cottage, Youlgrave, *c*. 1892.

Youlgrave village in quieter days, *c.* 1900. On the right is the old hall.

Holywell Lane, formerly Holloway Lane, Youlgrave, *c.* 1892. According to a local informant, the children may well be members of the Brassington family, who sold milk in those days.

Well-dressing at Back Top Well, Youlgrave, 1927. The designer was Will Yates. Back row, left to right: Gladys Nuttall, Frances Yates, Phyllis Birds, Alice Evans, Vernon Bacon, George Oldfield, Albert Shimwell. Front row: Jack Birds, Raymond Birds.

Another well-dressing scene with the local brass band in attendance, 1920s.

A dray leads the victory celebrations procession through the village in 1919.

The 9th Duke of Rutland and party pose beside the dressed well at the Reading Room, *c.* 1930.

Youlgrave Village Hall, given by Mrs Waterhouse of Lomberdale and the Misses Melland of Raenstor Close, was built in 1909. It houses the annual pantomime, which was started by Mr and Mrs Mocket before the war and has been famous locally for many years. Here, Widow Twankey, played by the late Tom Rhodes, is engaged in a little dollying in *Aladdin* in 1966. Left to right: Tom Rhodes, John Roper, Martin Brooke-Taylor, Jack Goodwin.

The Passion play *Noah and the Flood* at Youlgrave Women's Institute, 1937. Back row, left to right: Florence Lomas, Margaret Ollerenshaw, Bertha Frost, Marjorie Lomas (now Shimwell), Florence Birds, Ida Smith. Front row: Kathleen Toft, Elsie Lomas, Winnie Ogden.

This looks like a gathering of one of Youlgrave's friendly societies at the Bull's Head yard, Youlgrave, probably before the First World War. There were at least four societies in Youlgrave: the Buffaloes, the Foresters, the Oddfellows and (for teetotallers) the Rechabites. It is unlikely that this group outside the pub consisted of Rechabites. Back row, left to right: Ralph Webster, Ben Oldfield, Dan Prime, Frank Wragg, E. Wragg, Billy ('Becca') Oldfield, Joe Thornhill, -?-, Joe Johnson. Front row: Tom Coates, Will Hollis, Billy Smith, John Gould, Will ('Trotty') Birds, Fred Oldfield.

Akeroyd's quarry, Birchover, *c.* 1900. Birchover village is not far from Youlgrave. The men pictured here are making a pulpit, using only pickaxes. On the far left is Stephen Rowland Shimwell and on the far right is Charlie Wragg.

The Silver Jubilee celebrations outside the village hall in Youlgrave, 1935. The Misses Melland are giving out Jubilee cups and saucers to local children. Back row, left to right: Sam H. Evans, John Dale, Mrs Clara Taylor, F.G. Nuttall, G.H. Ollerenshaw, H. Lees, H. Colman, Mrs Gertrude Wragg, Les Wild, Harold Shimwell, Tom Cassels. Front row: Alice Wragg (Elliott), -?-, -?-, Miss M.H. Melland, Brian Colman, Miss Melland, Muriel Wragg.

Youlgrave church choir, 1954. Back row, left to right: H. Wragg, N. Brassington, H. Moss, G. Kenworth, N. Lever, J. Rowland. Middle row: Mrs Evans, Miss Oxley, G. Cresh, R. Garratt, H. Holland, -?-, Miss Oxley, ? Twyford, S. Boden. Front row: B. Buxton, -?-, K. Gladwin, B. Evans, Revd Mr Hadfield, H. Lees, P. Needham, ? Needham, A. Robinson. Seated: Brian Moss, Billy Oldfield, Peter Dawson, John Boden, Eric Billinge, Alan Cawley.

Youlgrave Horticultural Society show, 1951. Back row, left to right: B.G. Flood, A. Evans, J. Rowland, D. Wardle (judge), Bill Shimwell (judge), E. Lomas, W. Brooke-Taylor. Front row: Billy Hill, J. Fearn, R. Hill, Edith Bacon, A. Bacon, H. Cavendish, M. Shimwell, Florence Lomas, G. Crisp.

Youlgrave junior football club, 1947–8. Back row, left to right: Stuart Nuttall, Peter Colman, Alan Shimwell, Ivor Bacon. Middle row: Bert Marsden (manager), Leonard Gladwin, R. Wardle, Aaron Taylor (trainer). Seated: Charlie Hollis, Brian Frost, B. Broomhead, Rex Bacon, D. Birds.

Many older residents will remember steam lorries. This one was owned by the Longrake Spar Co. of Youlgrave. This firm is still in business.

An anniversary tea was held at Youlgrave's Wesleyan Reform Chapel to mark the centenary year in 1957. The chapel had been built on land provided by W.P. Thornhill and was opened in 1857. Its schoolroom was built in about 1860 and electric light was installed in 1906. Left to right: Mrs Evelyn Wood, Mrs Charlotte Walker, Mrs Nuttall, Revd C. Finnemore, Mr Arnold Prince, Mr Herbert Evans, Mr Leslie Wild, Mr Gregory Hadfield. The little girl is Avril Fryer.

Boys' Life Brigade, Youlgrave, *c.* 1906. The Brigade was started in Youlgrave by Angus McIver, the minister in charge of Youlgrave Congregational Church. After his departure, J. Dale and F. Bateman took over the work. The headquarters were at the village hall, and Bible classes were held weekly; camps were held at Sutton-on-Sea. Back row, left to right: Herbert Evans, Billy Toft, Harry Wardle, Gilbert Birds, Jim Birds, Lawrence Birds, Jim Lomas, Albert Birds, -?-. Middle row: Angus McIver (?), Billy Birds, Vernon Shimwell, Vic Toft, -?-, Billy Cook, -?-, Tommy Wardle, -?-, -?-. Front row: C.H. Johnson, Ted Lomas, -?-, -?-, G.W. Oldfield, G.H. Birds, -?-, Luther Shimwell, Len Hollis, -?-.

ROWSLEY & HADDON

Rowsley lies some 4 miles south of Bakewell and is divided by the A6. Great Rowsley, the older part, is a well-maintained village on the Duke of Rutland's estate, with seventeenth- and eighteenth-century stone houses. Little Rowsley was dominated by Rowsley station and its goods yard. Much of the property there was owned by the Midland Railway, which arrived in 1849. Here four young people pose for the photographer on the island in the middle of Rowsley Square opposite the Peacock Hotel.

Walter Howard, with yoke and buckets, standing with Stanley Wright and Mrs Howard, in Church Lane, Rowsley, *c.* 1910.

Farm workers at Rowsley, *c.* 1910. Standing, left to right: Mr Wall, Mrs Wall, -?-, Fred Elliott, -?-, -?-.

This postcard of Candwell's Mill, Rowsley, was produced by F.W. Whitehead. Built in 1875, it was powered by a water turbine first installed in 1898. Some of its grain was brought by railway from Liverpool. The mill is now a working museum.

A fine team of horses belonging to Mr Shimwell of Home Farm, pictured in Church Lane, Rowsley.

The Peacock Hotel, Rowsley, 1920s. Originally built as a private house by John Stevenson, agent to the Manners family at Haddon, in 1652, it became an inn many years ago.

The Wall family of Bridge House Farm, Rowsley, with their wagonette, which was used to transport many of the tourists arriving at Rowsley station for Chatsworth.

This is an intriguing postcard from about 1905. Obviously someone very important – perhaps royalty – is arriving at Rowsley station. The message written on the reverse suggests that the female arrival is of more interest than her consort. Rowsley station regularly saw the arrivals and departures of the king and queen, foreign royalty and VIPs over the years.

Rowsley engine shed, 1910. The original terminus of 1849 was beyond the road bridge by the house on the right. Just visible on the left is the new station of 1862 which opened when the line moved northwards. This photograph was taken by 'Photo Joe' (Joe Elliott), a Midland Railway guard, who took several of the pictures used in this section of the book.

The Peacock Hotel, Rowsley. Standing at the side door of the hotel (which led to the taproom) are, left to right, Ted Elliott, Arthur Howard, Harry Skinner, Tom Howsley, Hezekiah Gilbert, Jack Sutton, Ida Billingham, -?-.

Church Lane, Rowsley. The demolition of the railway bridge in the centre of the picture was one of the conditions for the sale of the track-bed in 1985, but if Peak Rail extends its line to Buxton a new girder bridge will have to be built here.

A cart passing under the same railway bridge, *c.* 1920. Bramwell, fruiterer of Buxton Road, Bakewell, delivered people's shopping to their house.

St Katherine's Church, Rowsley. It was built in 1855 to a design by Anthony Salvin junior.

Before hygiene regulations became stricter, many villages had a small tearoom catering for ramblers and cyclists. This wooden tearoom stood in Church Lane. Miss Hensburgh is looking over the wall.

The Misses Hensburgh take a rest from gardening, perhaps during the First World War.

A timeless view of Church Lane.

This is actually Chatsworth Road in Little Rowsley, despite the caption on the card! On the left are railway houses; the nearest date from 1896, the next are 1849–50, while the terrace of twenty-five was built in 1886–7. The last building is the Primitive Methodist chapel of 1902 designed by D.M. Wildgoose.

The large booking hall at Rowsley station specially prepared for the reception of King Edward VII and Queen Alexandra – no doubt these smart furnishings were returned to the company's headquarters in Derby to be used for the next royal visit.

Members of the Amalgamated Society of Railway Servants passing the Peacock Hotel, Rowsley. The ASRS was formed in 1872 and amalgamated with other unions to form the NUR in 1909.

St Elphin's girls eagerly await the arrival of King George V and Queen Mary at Rowsley station in July 1933.

The royal train departing from Rowsley for London Euston in July 1933. All eight vehicles were of London & North Western Railway origin and were still painted in the colours of that company instead of the more familiar maroon livery of the LMS. The Express Dairy Co. factory had only recently been opened, using the railway to despatch its products.

Built in the middle ages, Haddon Hall ceased to be lived in during the time of John, 3rd Duke of Rutland (1721–79) and was 'abandoned' for about 200 years, although it was never left empty. Restoration began in 1912 and continued until the end of the 1920s.

The cottage by the entrance to Haddon Hall. Its garden, though small, was always magnificent.

The Long Gallery at Haddon Hall (wrongly captioned on this postcard as the Ballroom) was 110 ft long and 17 ft wide. The room was panelled and the present ceiling put up after the marriage of John Manners (1567–1611) and Dorothy Vernon.

The kitchen at Haddon Hall is of great size, about 28 ft by 24 ft, although it is low-ceilinged and dark. There are numerous larders, store rooms and pantries.

The 9th Duke of Rutland (1852–1925). Before the sales of 1920 the Dukes of Rutland owned most of Bakewell and much of the land around; they still own most of Alport, Haddon and Great Rowsley.

The 10th Duke of Devonshire (1895–1949). He was president of Bakewell Show in 1921 and 1949.

A winter party at Chatsworth. The original photograph was given to Mrs Wilson of the Pudding Shop in Bakewell in 1910 by Miss Underwood, daughter of the Duke of Rutland's agent, who is sitting next to King Edward VII in the picture.

May Booth (later Elliot) and her mother, Thyrza Booth, at Edensor. Mrs Thyrza Booth was appointed postmistress at Edensor in August 1857.

A railway through Chatsworth? It was built in connection with the construction of the Derwent Water Board's reservoirs, when an aqueduct was provided to convey the water. A 3 ft gauge line ran from Rowsley through the park for six months in 1906 to transport building material and pipes. By agreement it was quickly dismantled after the need for it had ceased.

A Down (northbound) freight train being banked by a Class 2F 0–6–0 locomotive north of Haddon Tunnel, August 1933. Banking was introduced to ease the strain on couplings and prevent breakaways on rising gradients. Shale cutting is visible in the distance.

ACKNOWLEDGEMENTS

Producing a book of this kind depends very much on the generosity and help of local people and there are in consequence many to be thanked. Foremost of these is Laurence Knighton, without whose extensive collection of Bakewell pictures this book would have been impossible, and without whose detailed knowledge of the town and its buildings the book would have been less informative and less accurate.

Sincere thanks are due to the following, who gave advice and lent photographs:

Mrs J. Andrews, Youlgrave · Mrs A. Axe, Bakewell CofE School · Bakewell Town Council · Mr K. Banbrook, Lady Manners' School · Mr L. Birds, Southport · Mrs Bradley, Derby · BR (LMR) Euston · Mr E. Charlesworth, Bakewell · Mr R. Corkill, Peacock Players, Bakewell · *Derbyshire Times*, Chesterfield · Mr J. Dunsford, Bakewell · Mrs I. Evans, Youlgrave · Mr and Mrs B. Eyre, Rowsley · Mr R. Fox, Bakewell · Miss A. Gilman, Youlgrave · Mr M. Hargreaves, St Anselm's School, Bakewell · Miss R. Hughes, MRCVS, Bakewell · Mrs J. Jones, Wirksworth · Mrs R. Lea, Bakewell Museum · Mr J. McCrindle, Ashford · *Matlock Mercury* · Mr F. Morton, Darley Dale · Mr E. Paulson, Darley Dale · Mr P. Robinson, Bakewell · Mrs E. Salomoni, Bakewell · Miss A. Sellors, Bakewell · *Sheffield Telegraph* · Mr W. Shimwell, Youlgrave · Mr D. Vardy, Darley Dale · Mr G. Waite, Totley · Mr and Mrs T. Walker, Alport · Mrs J. Walvin, Bakewell Show Office · Mrs B. Wilde, Bakewell.

Finally, thanks as always to Gwyneth Barton, both for her encouragement, her powers of organization and the constant supply of tea and sandwiches.

Derbyshire Library Services maintains a large collection of photographic material relating to the county, which is held in the Local Studies Library at Derby and the County Library Headquarters in the County Hall at Matlock. If anyone has any old photographs of the county which could be donated or lent for copying, your local library would be pleased to see them.

David A. Barton
Darley Dale
April 1997

BRITAIN IN OLD PHOTOGRAPHS

To order any of these titles please telephone our distributor, Littlehampton Book Services on 01903 721596
For a catalogue of these and our other titles please ring Regina Schinner on 01453 731114